The Force Multiplier Model

Designing Outcomes When Money Can't Lead

J. SAUCEDO

Copyright © 2026 J. Saucedo

The Force Multiplier Model

All rights reserved.

Company names listed are used for illustrative purposes only and do not imply endorsement or affiliation.

ISBN: 9798244036152

TABLE OF CONTENTS

	Acknowledgments	i
	Introduction	iii
	How To Read This Book	vi
1	Sponsorship Is Broken	1
2	The Small-Budget Trap	7
3	Value Exists Before Cash	13
4	The Force Multiplier Principal	19
5	Collaborative Exchange	27
6	Why Sports Is the Distribution Layer	35
7	The Community Engine	43
8	Why Systems Beat Deals	51
9	Why This Works Without You	57
10	Who Already Has What This Requires	65
11	Why Resistance Always Shows Up	71
12	Leading Without Chasing	77
13	When the System Becomes the Advantage	83
14	Scaling Down Is the Proof	87
15	The Shift That Changes Everything	91
	Seeing the Pattern	97
	Afterword	101
	About the Author	105

ACKNOWLEDGMENTS

This work is the result of years spent building alongside others.

To the players, coaches, cheerleaders, volunteers, supporters, and collaborators who showed up – season after season, in visible moments and quiet ones – thank you. The lessons in this book weren't learned in isolation. They were shaped through shared effort, long days, difficult decisions, and the steady commitment of people who chose to be part of something even when outcomes were uncertain.

There were highs and lows. Wins and losses. Momentum and setbacks. None of it would have mattered without people worth going through it with. The trust, patience, and belief you extended made it possible to keep going long enough to recognize the patterns this book describes.

The book exists because of what we built together – and because of what we were willing to learn along the way.

INTRODUCTION

This book didn't start as a book.

It started as a pattern.

For more than two decades, I ran programs with limited resources, inconsistent conditions, and very little margin for error. Every season looked different. Every challenge arrived unannounced. There was no roadmap. No master plan. No formal training that told me what to do next.

And yet, it kept working.

Not perfectly. Not easily. But consistently.

For a long time, I didn't have language for what I was doing. I trusted it because I had to. When you don't have money to rely on, you either learn how to think differently — or you stop moving altogether.

This book is an attempt to name that way of thinking.

Let's be clear about something early.

This is not a fundraising book.
It's not a sports book.
And it's not a collection of clever tactics.

Sports simply provides a clean environment to see the mechanics clearly. The same principles apply to small businesses, entrepreneurs, youth programs, and anyone trying to build something without the luxury of excess capital.

This book is about **how outcomes are designed when money cannot lead the conversation.**

Money matters.

Financial freedom matters.
Stability matters.
Growth matters.

Anyone who says otherwise isn't being honest.

But money is not the starting point most people think it is.

The phrase *"it takes money to make money"* is often repeated without nuance. What people usually mean is that money makes things easier once a structure already exists. What they rarely explain is **how that structure gets built in the first place**.

This book lives in that gap.

Many people reach this point after doing everything they were taught to do.

They worked. They raised families. They carried responsibility through economic shifts that compressed savings and increased pressure everywhere. What little margin existed was often absorbed by life itself, not mismanagement.

What's rarely acknowledged is that almost none of this is taught. Not in school. Not in college. Not in the places that claim to prepare people for business. Instead, most people are handed theory, policy, or credentials — and then expected to translate that into real-world execution on their own.

When they finally try to move forward — to build something, to formalize an idea, or to seek support — they often encounter systems that weren't designed for where they actually are. The criteria make sense on paper, but they don't reflect real operating conditions. The result isn't guidance — it's doubt.

In that moment, it's easy to assume the idea is wrong. Or that they're early, unprepared, or unrealistic.

This book starts from a different assumption: that many early operators aren't wrong — they're simply operating ahead of the language, and outside systems that were never built to reflect how business actually gets started.

This system wasn't developed in abundance.
It was developed in constraint.

That's why beginners often grasp it faster than experienced operators who've been trained to lead with spend, scale, or speed.

If you're early, underfunded, or feeling pressure to "figure it out," you're not behind. You're in a position to see leverage that others miss.

This book doesn't reward cleverness.
It rewards discipline.

Years after developing this approach through instinct and repetition, I began reading books by operators who had reached far higher levels of success. I noticed something interesting.

They were describing the same mechanics — just from the other side of the equation.

The difference was not intelligence or access.
It was timing and language.

That recognition didn't give me confidence.
It confirmed it.

This book is written so others don't have to wait years for that confirmation.

It will not:
- Motivate you with stories of overnight success
- Give you scripts or shortcuts
- Promise results without resistance
- Teach you how to "hack" growth

Those things don't hold under pressure.

What does hold is structure.

HOW TO READ THIS BOOK

This book is intentionally restrained.

It doesn't chase energy, emotion, or entertainment. Not because those things are bad — but because they distract from the mechanics.

The chapters are written to be clear rather than expressive, direct rather than persuasive. Ideas are introduced once, tested, and then built upon. There is very little repetition by design.

This isn't meant to impress you.
It's meant to orient you.

If you read it quickly, it will still make sense.
If you read it slowly, it will likely change how you see things around you.

Either way, the value is not in agreement.
It's in recognition.

If you're ready to look at what you already have differently, turn the page.

1 SPONSORSHIP IS BROKEN

Most businesses don't say it out loud, but they feel it.

They've written checks.
They've put logos on banners.
They've sponsored events, teams, tournaments, and programs.

And afterward, when asked what they got in return, the answer is usually vague.

"Exposure"
"Brand awareness"
"Goodwill."

None of those show up on a balance sheet. None of them help when budgets tighten.

So sponsorships become the first thing cut – not because businesses don't care, but because the value was never clearly defined in the first place.

This is not failure of generosity.
It's a failure of structure.

Traditional sponsorship models are built on a simple assumption:
If people see your logo enough times, value is being created.

That assumption may have worked when:

- Media channels were limited
- Attention was centralized
- Audiences had fewer choices

But that world no longer exists.
Today:

- Attention is fragmented
- Logos are ignored
- Visibility does not equal engagement

Most sponsorships are sold as *placement*, not participation.
And placement alone is passive.
Passive inputs produce passive returns.

This model hurts everyone – but it punishes small businesses the most.
Large brands can afford:

- Repetition
- Long timelines
- Soft returns

Small businesses cannot.

When a local business spends $2,500 or $5,000 on a sponsorship, it's not a marketing experiment. It's a risk.

They don't need more impressions.
They need outcomes.

And when those outcomes are unclear, the decision is easy:
"Sponsorship doesn't work."

What they really mean is:
"This version of sponsorship doesn't work for us."

Minor league and community sports programs didn't invent this problem, but they feel it the hardest.

They're told to:

- Sell signage
- Sell logos
- Sell exposure

So they do.

And then they wonder why:

- Partners churn
- Budgets fluctuate
- Relationships stay transactional

When sponsorship is reduced to advertising inventory, the relationship ends when the money does.

That's not partnership.
That's a rental agreement.

Here's the core issue:
Traditional sponsorships treat money as the only meaningful input.
But money is just one form of value.

Time has value.
Labor has value.
Reach has value.
Trust has value.
Facilities have value.
Access has value.

When those assets are ignored, the system becomes inefficient and –
And fragile.

At some point, it becomes clear that the problem isn't effort or intent. It's the structure itself. Once you see the pattern, it's hard to unsee it.

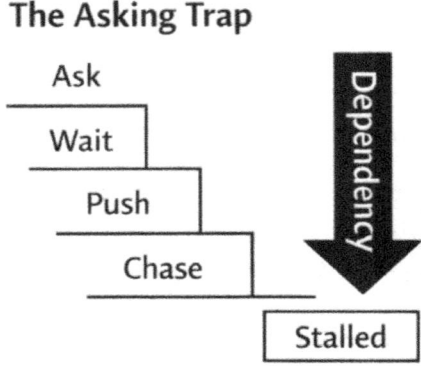

Case Story: When Exposure Wasn't Enough

A local organization sought sponsors to support a growing program. Budgets were tight on both sides.

Sponsors were asked to contribute cash in exchange for logo placement. Engagement was low. Retention was inconsistent.

- The organization had scheduled events and community trust
- Partners had staff, networks, and operational capacity
- None of these were being exchanged

The model remained cash-for-placement.

Short-term support, long-term disengagement.

When sponsorship ignores non-cash assets, value remains trapped on both sides.

Instead of asking:
"How much can you give?"

A better question is:
"What can we build together?"

That single shift changes:

- Who can participate
- How value is measured
- Why relationships last

It's the difference between buying space and sharing outcomes.

If sponsorship is broken, the solution is not to abandon it.
The solution is to **rebuild it around execution instead of exposure**.

In the next chapter, we'll examine why well-intentioned partners get trapped in small budgets – and how a different structure unlocks participation without requiring bigger checks.

THE FORCE MULTIPLIER MODEL

2 THE SMALL-BUDGET TRAP

Why Good Partners Are Locked Out by Cash-First Models

Most sponsorship models don't fail because businesses don't care.
They fail because the rules are wrong.
The traditional model assumes support must start with a check.
If there's no budget line item, the conversation ends.

That single assumption quietly eliminates the very partners who:

- Care the most
- Are closest to the community
- Would benefit the most from alignment
- And could contribute real value if asked differently
- This is the small-budget trap.
- Not a lack of goodwill.
- A lack of options.

Small businesses don't think in "sponsorship tiers."
They think in:

- Payroll
- Inventory
- Time
- Relationships
- Capacity

When they hear:

"Sponsorships start at $2,500."

What they really hear is:
"This isn't for you."

Even when they *want* to help.
Even when they *believe* in the mission.
Even when they already spend that much every month—just not in cash they can hand over.

The model excludes them even before value is discussed.

The issue isn't willingness. It's structure. Most partnerships fail not because people don't want help, but because the only option offered was donation.

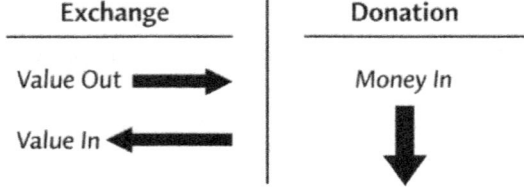

Case Story: "The $1000 We Didn't Ask For"

During one off-season, our team earned the opportunity to play at Dallas Cowboys Stadium. To secure the game, we had a ticket sales requirement we were about **$1000 short** of reaching. In a small market like ours, most sponsorships ranged from **$100 to $400**, and it was a slower time of year for most businesses.

We reached out to several of our strongest partners to see if anyone could help close the gap. Each conversation was positive, but consistent. They were supportive, but unable to contribute additional cash on short notice.

One business owner stood out. He owned two establishments we already worked closely with:

- A buffet restaurant our players frequented
- A sports bar where we hosted meet-and-greets, sent opposing teams to eat after games, played our road game streams and used for a team meeting place.

He always sponsored modestly, about $150 per location, and supported us in ways that didn't show up on an invoice: promotion, access, and hospitality.

When asked directly about additional sponsorship, he politely declined. Not because he didn't want to help, but because, at the moment, he couldn't.

What the cash-first conversation missed:

- Two food-service operations
- Existing staff and kitchen capacity
- A trusted relationship with our audience
- Flexibility during off-hours
- Willingness to support the team creatively

None of that fit into a standard sponsorship package.

Instead of pushing for a check, we proposed a different option: **a ticketed plate sale**.

The team would:
- Pre-sell meal tickets
- Handle promotion
- Manage distribution and delivery

The restaurant would:
- Prepare limited number of meals
- Choose the timing and constraints

The owner set clear boundaries:

- Tuesday lunch only (when the bar was normally closed)
- A cap of **100 plates**
- A simple, familiar cheeseburger meal
- No dine-in, we would handle delivery

We agreed to proceed without even defining the revenue split in advance, relying on trust built over years.

The team pre-sold all 100 plates to the larger, nearby employers, within a week. The event ran smoothly. At the end of the day, we asked to settle the split.

The owner said:
"The team keeps it all."

He explained that at cost, the 100 plates matched what he typically spent on the team's sponsorship across the year and considered it his sponsorship for the upcoming season.

The team cleared the shortfall.
The game at Dallas Cowboys Stadium moved forward.
The relationship deepened.
The following season, we formally earmarked a **$1000 sponsorship package** for his businesses, reflecting the real value exchanged.

Cash-first models lock out partners who are willing but temporarily constrained.

Cash is only one form of value.
But it's treated as the only *acceptable* one.

This creates three systemic problems:

- **It filters out alignment partners early.** The businesses closest to community are often the most cash-constrained.

- **It underutilized real assets.** Facilities, services, labor, reach, and credibility go unused.

- **It caps total impact.** Cash-only thinking limits scale to whoever can write checks.

The result is fewer partners, weaker ties, and shallow outcomes.

The better question is not:
"How much can you sponsor?"

It's:
"What do you already have that helps us win?"

When value is defined broadly:

- Businesses stop self-eliminating
- Conversations open instead of close
- Partnerships become collaborative instead of transactional

Cash often follows—but it doesn't have to lead.

Sports organizations don't just need funding.
They need:

- Infrastructure
- Services
- Reach
- Credibility
- Stability

Small businesses can provide all of that—if the model lets them in.
The irony is that the organizations that need the most support, often run the most respective partnership systems.

When good partners are locked out:

- Programs stay under funded
- Communities stay disconnected
- Opportunities stay small

Not because the support isn't there—but because the invitation is poorly designed.

What Comes Next

If cash isn't the only entry point...

What does a **better partnership model** actually look like?

One that:

- Expands access
- Increases total value
- And produces measurable outcomes

That's where we go next.

3 VALUE EXISTS BEFORE CASH

Why Assets Matter More Than Budgets

The mistake most partnership conversations make is not asking for money.

It's asking for money **first**.
Cash is the easiest thing to quantify, so it becomes the default gatekeeper.
But ease of measurement is not the same as importance.
Value exists long before a check is written.

Every organization already operates with assets, whether they recognize them or not.

Assets include:

- Labor
- Space
- Time
- Access
- Audience
- Trust
- Schedule certainty
- Operational capability

Most of these never appear on a balance sheet.
But they drive outcomes every day.
When partnerships are framed narrowly, these assets stay idle.

Cash-first models persist because:

- They're simple
- They're fast
- They reduce negotiation

But they also:

- Shrink the partner pool
- Limit creativity
- Reduce total value created

Cash solves *one* problem well.
It doesn't solve *every* problem best.

Case Story: Using What Was Already There All Along

In the first year of launching a football program in a rural market, we initially approached what we believed would be larger budget sponsors. One of those conversations led to a small regional shopping mall in a nearby town, about 75% occupied, anchored by a movie theater, and actively working to maintain foot traffic during a challenging retail period.

The mall manager was supportive of the program but explained early that she did not have the authority or the budget to sponsor financially.

In a traditional sponsorship model, that would have ended the discussion.
Instead, the conversation continued.

As we walked through the season timeline, we mentioned that while football tryouts happen shortly before the season kickoff, cheer auditions take place nearly six months in advance to allow time for training and performance preparation.

The mall manager immediately saw the opportunity.

She had:

- An empty storefront
- Consistent daily foot traffic
- A space already designed with sports-themed visuals, including a football field graphic on the floor

These were assets sitting idle for months.

Rather than centering the partnership on sponsorship dollars, the exchange was built around **early-season activation**.

The mall offered:

- Use of the empty storefront for cheer auditions
- Ongoing access to the space for cheer practices for six months leading into the season
- Permission to promote the program throughout the mall during the entire period

The mall also became the **recognized brand partner** for the cheer squad for the full season.

An adjacent western wear store joined organically, partnering with the cheerleaders for a themed photoshoot that produced promotional posters.

For six months leading up to football tryouts:

- Cheer practices became a visible, recurring activation in a high-traffic location
- Shoppers routinely stopped to watch, ask questions, and engage with the program
- Awareness of the team began building well before traditional football tryouts
- Interest extended beyond fans and potential football players stopped to inquire as well

- The mall activated vacant space and increased dwell time
- Retail partners gained content and seasonal relevance

No cash changed hands.
Momentum did.

When unused assets are activated early, awareness compounds long before money enters the conversation.

Cash-First vs. Structure-First Sequence

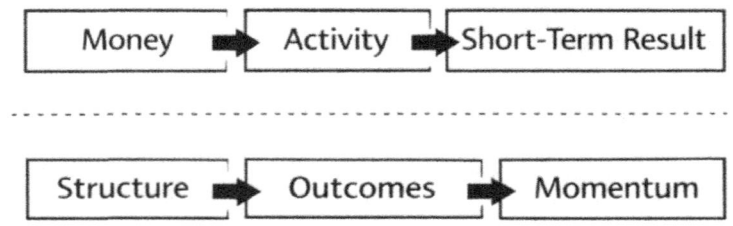

The Shift That Changes Everything

The most productive partnerships don't start with:
"What's your budget?"

They start with:
"What do you already have to work with?"

That single shift:

- Lowers friction
- Invites creativity
- Expands participation
- It can even create momentum

And most importantly, it changes the psychology of the relationship.
The partner is no longer a donor.
They are an operator.

Sports programs already control:

- Attention
- Schedule
- Emotion
- Community trust

When paired with business assets, the combination creates leverage neither side can buy alone.

This is where the force multiplier begins to form.

What Comes Next

If value exists before cash…

How do you **design partnerships that intentionally stack assets** instead of chasing checks?

That's the system.
And that's where we go next.

4 THE FORCE MULTIPLIER PRINCIPLE

Why Shared Execution Beats Solo Effort

By this point, one thing should be clear:
Most partnership models fail not because people lack resources, but because those resources are never combined.

They stay isolated.

Businesses operate alone.
Sports programs operate alone.
Community organizations operate alone.

Each does what it can within its own constraints.

The Force Multiplier Principle explains why that approach will always underperform.

A force multiplier is simple:

When aligned entities act together, the combined outcome is greater than the sum of individual efforts.

This isn't theoretical.
It's operational.

In partnerships, the multiplier doesn't come from money.

It comes from **shared execution**.

When organizations act independently:

- Impact scales linearly
- Resources are duplicated
- Effort competes instead of compounds

A business spends on advertising.
A sports program spends on operations.
A nonprofit spends on outreach.

Each pays full price for partial results.

No one benefits from the overlap.

Shared execution looks different.

Instead of asking:
"What can each of us afford to do alone?"

The question becomes:
"What happens if we do this together?"

When execution is shared:

- One action serves multiple goals
- One audience serves multiple partners
- One effort produces multiple returns

That's the multiplier.

This is where sports becomes more than entertainment.

Sports programs already control:

- Attention
- Schedule
- Emotion
- Community gathering

Those elements are difficult to buy and impossible to fake.

When a sports program partners operationally with a business:

- The business doesn't need to create attention
- It plugs into existing attention

That's leverage.

This is important.

The force multiplier is not:

- A discount
- A bundle
- A barter deal
- A creative sponsorship package

Those still treat value as transactional.

The multiplier only appears when:

- Execution overlaps
- Outcomes are shared
- Incentives align

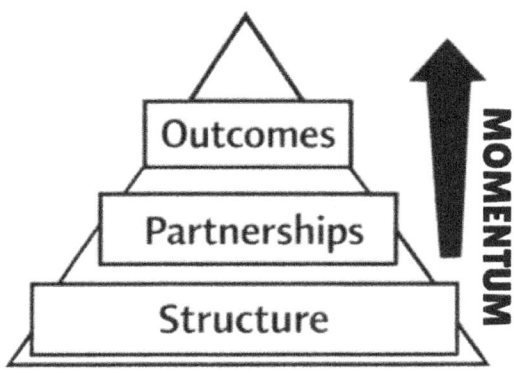

Case Story: The Sports Bar Traffic Multiplier

Early on, we learned the hard way that we are a football team — not a food truck.

Trying to operate outside our core competency created risk, friction, and reputational exposure we didn't need.

From that point forward, we approached fundraising differently.

Instead of trying to do everything ourselves, we started looking for partners who already did certain things better than we ever could.

That realization shaped what came next.

The team needed offseason revenue and continued visibility.

Local businesses already had traffic, food credibility, and operational infrastructure—but those assets were being used independently.

The team worked to build attention.
The business worked to serve customers.

The efforts overlapped, but they weren't coordinated.

- A well-known sports bar with:
1. Established food reputation
2. High daily traffic
3. Large in-house sports audience
4. On-site entertainment (TVs, pool tables, darts, volleyball courts)

- A football team with:
1. A loyal supporter base
2. Players and staff willing to execute
3. Branded apparel and visibility
4. Content and storytelling capability

The audience was already shared.
The execution was not.

Instead of the team attempting to run food operations, the partnership was structured so each side did what it already did well.

- The sports bar prepared brisket plates at cost during a defined lunch window

- The team handled ticket presales and on-site distribution
- Revenue was split by agreement
- Ticket holders who stayed to eat received a free iced tea

No new infrastructure was created.
Existing systems were aligned.

The results went beyond ticket revenue.

- Plates sold consistently
- Many attendees stayed, ordered appetizers, and increased average spend

- Regular customers interacted with players and staff wearing team apparel

- Conversations about the team happened organically in a high-traffic setting

One activation:

- Generated fundraising revenue
- Drove incremental food and beverage sales
- Built awareness and affinity
- Strengthened the partner relationship

The effort didn't add up.
It multiplied.

Over time, the partnership expanded.

In one offseason, the sports bar donated court time for a volleyball tournament:

- Participants paid entry fees
- Prizes were sourced through gift cards
- The event was filmed and distributed on social media

This created offseason content, engagement, and visibility—without football games being played.

The same partnership produced:

- Revenue
- Content
- Community engagement
- Momentum

When execution overlaps, one action can replace multiple separate efforts — and outperform them all.

The force multiplier doesn't require:

- More money
- More staff
- More complexity

It requires **coordination**.

That's why this model works in:

- Small towns
- Rural markets
- Cash-constrained environments

And why it often outperforms larger budget efforts that lack alignment.

This is the key realization:
Multipliers don't happen by accident.
They are designed.
They appear when partnerships are built around:

- Execution, not placement
- Assets, not budgets
- Outcomes, not exposure

That design choice is what separates:

- Sponsors from partners
- Support from leverage
- Activity from impact

What Comes Next

If shared execution is the engine…

Then the next question is obvious:

How do you intentionally stack multiple partners so the multiplier compounds?

That's the system.

And that's where we go next.

THE FORCE MULTIPLIER MODEL

5 COLLABORATIVE EXCHANGE

The Invisible Economy Most Organizations Ignore

By now, it should be clear that money is not the only thing moving in a partnership.

What's less obvious—and far more important—is that most value is exchanged **without ever being priced.**

That value still matters.
It just isn't labeled.

This is the invisible economy.

Collaborative exchange is not barter.

It is not "you do this, I'll do that."

And it is not a workaround for lack of cash.

Collaborative exchange is the **intentional alignment of non-cash assets toward shared outcomes.**

The goal isn't fairness by invoice.
The goal is leverage by design.

Most organizations are trained to recognize only what they can:

- Price
- Invoice
- Depreciate
- Expense

Anything else gets treated as secondary.

But consider what actually drives outcomes:

- Time
- Labor
- Access
- Trust
- Space
- Attention
- Scheduling priority

None of these appear neatly on a balance sheet.
All of them move results.

When they go unrecognized, they go unused.

When partnerships are framed only around money:

- Conversations narrow early
- Creativity disappears
- Participation drops
- Outcomes flatten

The model becomes efficient—but fragile.

It works only when budgets are healthy.
It fails the moment conditions tighten.

That's why cash-first systems break under pressure.

When non-cash assets are acknowledged, something changes.

Instead of asking:

"What can you afford?"

The conversation becomes:

"What are you already doing that we can build on?"

That shift:

- Expands who can participate
- Increases total value created
- Reduces dependency on any single input

Most importantly, it turns partners into operators.

The Building Blocks of Collaborative Exchange
Every collaborative exchange is built from the same components.

They're just combined differently.

Common Non-Cash Assets Include:

- Facilities and space
- Staff time
- Existing audiences
- Distribution channels
- Scheduling control
- Credibility and trust
- Content and storytelling capacity

The mistake is treating these as "soft."
They're not.

They are **foundational**.

Case Story: The Value That Solved a Revenue Problem

A local professional broadcasting channel streamed high school sports year-round. Their business model depended on monthly advertiser renewals tied directly to the availability of live sports content.

During the school year, advertiser retention was strong.
Every summer, it wasn't.

Traditional Limitation
When school sports ended, the channel ran out of content. Advertisers dropped off, and the broadcaster had to spend time and money re-selling those same advertisers when the school year returned.

The problem wasn't advertiser interest.
It was a seasonal content gap.

Our football team already had:

- A full summer game schedule
- Live, local sports content
- Strong community recognition and goodwill
- Existing sponsor relationships
- Broadcast advertising inventory already built into its sponsorship packages

None of these assets required new spend.

Instead of charging for broadcast rights, the team allowed the channel to stream games at no cost.

The broadcaster tested whether filling the summer content gap would keep advertisers engaged through the offseason.

At the same time, the team's sponsors gained additional exposure through **broadcast ads already included in sponsorship packages**, extending value without increasing price.

- Advertisers stayed active year-round
- Seasonal churn was eliminated

- The broadcaster reduced time and cost spent re-selling ads
- The team gained professional live-stream coverage
- Sponsors received broadcast exposure without additional spend
- Sports bar partners were able to air away games live in their venues

No new invoices were created.
Existing assets carried the value.

When non-cash assets are treated as first-class inputs, partnerships stop waiting on budgets and start solving real problems.

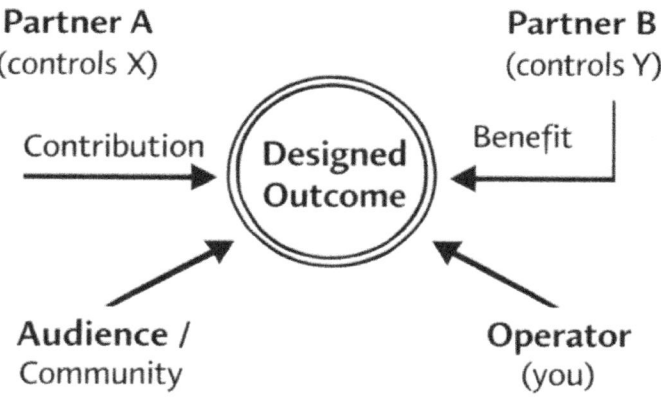

Why Sports Accelerates Collaborative Exchange
Sports programs are uniquely positioned in this economy.

They already concentrate:

- Attention
- Emotion
- Timing
- Community identity

That makes them powerful **exchange hubs**.
When a sports program partners through collaborative exchange:

- Businesses don't have to create attention
- They redirect it
- They don't buy trust
- They borrow it

This is why sports works as infrastructure—not just entertainment.

Collaborative exchange only works when:

- Expectations are clear
- Execution is shared
- Outcomes are defined

When it's vague, it feels like a favor.
When it's designed, it becomes a system.

The difference is intentionality.

At small scale, collaborative exchange feels intuitive.

At larger scale, it must be structured.

That's where most programs stall.

They know exchange works—but they don't know how to **stack it** across multiple partners without chaos.

That's the next step.

What Comes Next
If collaborative exchange is the fuel…

Then the question becomes:

How do you stack multiple partners so value compounds instead of competing?

That's the architecture.

And that's where we go next.

6 WHY SPORTS IS THE DISTRIBUTION LAYER

Attention, Timing, and Trust—Already Assembled

Most partnership models start with a problem:

How do we get attention?

Sports doesn't.

Sports starts with attention already concentrated.

That's the difference.

In business, distribution is almost always the most expensive problem to solve.

It takes time.
It takes money.
It takes repeated effort.

Most organizations spend the majority of their resources trying to:

- Get noticed
- Stay relevant
- Be remembered

Sports doesn't have to do that work from scratch.

It already has:

- Scheduled events
- Known dates
- Anticipation
- Built-in audiences

That makes sports a distribution layer—not just a product.

Sports aggregates attention in ways few things can.

People show up:

- At the same time
- In the same place
- For the same reason

That matters.
Attention isn't scattered.
It's synchronized.

When partners plug into that moment, they aren't chasing attention—they're **joining it**.

Timing Is Predictable
Most marketing efforts struggle with timing.

Sports doesn't.

Games are scheduled months in advance.
Seasons have rhythm.
Audiences know when to pay attention.

That predictability allows partners to:

- Plan
- Prepare
- Align resources

Predictable timing turns activation into execution instead of guesswork.

This part is often overlooked.

Sports programs—especially local and community-based ones—carry trust by default.

They represent:

- Youth pathways
- Community pride
- Shared identity
- Local effort

That trust isn't transferable in theory—but it is borrowable in practice.

When a business partners with a sports program:

- They don't have to explain who they are
- They don't have to justify why they care

They inherit credibility.

Collaborative exchange needs three things to work well:

1. Attention
2. Timing
3. Trust

Sports already has all three.

That's why:

- Non-cash assets perform better when routed through sports
- Partnerships activate faster
- Outcomes compound instead of stall

Sports become the hub, not the hero.

Borrowing Trust

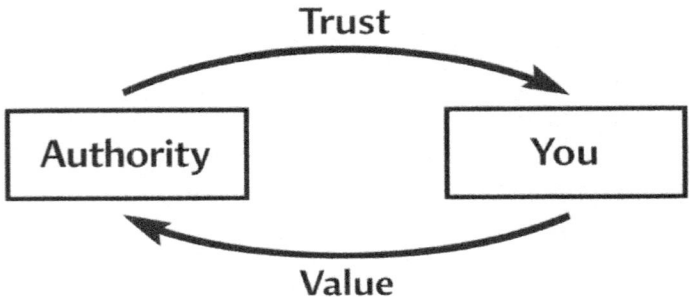

Case Story: When National Brands Routed Local Outreach Through A Local Sports Program

The Army All-American Bowl is a nationally televised, blue-chip high school all-star game. The event runs paid advertising to promote the game itself and maintains national visibility year after year.

That wasn't the challenge.

The challenge was delivering a **local youth football outreach event**—on short notice, outside the school calendar, and without launching a separate promotional campaign.

Reaching families at scale for a one-off youth camp normally requires:

- Paid local promotion
- School or league coordination
- Long lead times
- Multiple points of trust

For this event, none of that was available.

The Bowl's local outreach partner, Walmart, already knew something important:

Our team could deliver.

The football program already had:

- A trusted following among families
- Active social media channels that parents paid attention to
- Existing football equipment and staffing
- Credibility with youth athletes and parents
- The ability to mobilize participation quickly, even in our offseason

These assets didn't need to be built.
They were already in place.

Instead of spending to promote the outreach event, Walmart and the Army All-American Bowl routed it through our team.

The team:

- Promoted the youth camp through its existing channels
- Provided football equipment and on-site execution
- Delivered turnout without paid advertising

The Bowl provided:

- Branded shirts
- Prizes
- Permission to co-brand content

The event moved fast because it didn't need explanation.

The camp was delivered smoothly and on time.

- Kids attended
- Parents trusted the event
- Photos and video were captured and shared
- Co-branded content was distributed and tagged to national channels

The Bowl achieved its outreach goal without launching a new local campaign.

Walmart fulfilled its community engagement objective through a trusted local platform.

The team operated as the connector.

After the event, the Bowl's leadership treated the team as a sponsor, providing game tickets and seating at the sponsor banquet, reflecting how they viewed the value delivered.

Sports works as a distribution layer because trust and attention are already assembled—and can be activated faster than money can be deployed.

This is important.

Sports is not:

- Selling impressions
- Acting as an ad platform
- Replacing marketing departments

Sports is **reducing friction**.

It's shortening the distance between:

- Effort and outcome
- Intention and impact

Partnership and execution

At national scale, attention is abstract.
At the local level, it's personal.

People recognize:

- Jerseys
- Logos
- Faces

They show up because they care—not because they were targeted.

That's why local sports outperforms generic marketing for partnership-based models.

If sports is the distribution layer…

Then the next step is obvious:

How do you intentionally **stack multiple partners** around that layer without chaos?

That's not theory.
That's structure.

What Comes Next
If sports is the hub…

Then the question becomes:

How do you design a partnership system that scales without losing clarity or control?

That's the architecture.

And that's where we go next.

THE FORCE MULTIPLIER MODEL

7 THE PARTNERSHIP STACK

How to Build Leverage Without Chaos

At this point, one thing should be clear:

Partnerships don't fail because people don't want to collaborate. They fail because collaboration isn't designed.

Most organizations treat partnerships as one-off relationships. One sponsor. One deal. One activation.

That approach doesn't scale.

The Partnership Stack is how you move from **individual partnerships** to a **system of partnerships**—without losing clarity, control, or trust.

Flat partnerships all look the same:

- One logo
- One mention
- One benefit list

They exist in parallel, not in relation to one another.

That creates three problems:

1. Every partner competes for the same attention
2. The organization manages each relationship independently
3. Value plateaus quickly

No matter how many partners you add, outcomes stay linear.

That's not leverage.
That's load.

A partnership stack is a **layered system**, not a list.

Each partner:

- Plays a different role
- Contributes a different asset
- Receives value in a different way

But all partners are aligned around the **same distribution layer**.

The stack is designed so:

- No partner cannibalizes another
- One activation can serve multiple partners
- Value compounds as the stack grows

Every effective partnership stack has three layers.
Not because it's theoretical—but because it works.

1. Anchor Partners
Stability and Credibility

Anchor partners provide:

- Infrastructure
- Consistency
- Trust signals

They are not always the highest-paying partners.

They are the most **structurally important**.

Examples:

- Facilities
- Media
- Institutional brands
- Core service providers

Without anchors, everything else wobbles.

2. Activation Partners
Execution and Momentum

Activation partners bring:

- Capacity
- Participation
- Energy

They are closest to execution.

Examples:

- Restaurants
- Retailers
- Gyms
- Service businesses

They turn plans into action.

3. Amplification Partners
Reach and Reinforcement

Amplification partners extend:

- Visibility
- Validation
- Awareness

They don't need to execute the activation.
They make sure it's seen.

Examples:

- Media outlets
- Influencers
- Community organizations
- Digital platforms

They help outcomes travel further than effort alone.

The stack works because:

- Each partner has a clear role
- No one is asked to do everything
- Value flows through the system, not just to one party

One activation can:

- Use an anchor's infrastructure
- Be executed by activation partners
- Be extended by amplification partners

That's how one action produces multiple outcomes.

Case Story: When Roles Were Clear, Participation Followed

For several years, the team held a Holiday Benefit Exhibition Game. From the team's perspective, the game served a very practical purpose. It functioned as the final live-action evaluation for players coming out of fall tryouts before the program paused for the holidays and resumed training in January.

The game needed to happen regardless.
The question was whether it could do more than serve the team.

When the event was first considered as a benefit game, the risk was familiar: too many parties, too many interests, and no clear structure. Charity events often fall apart not because people don't care, but because no one is sure who is responsible for what.

Without clarity, participation becomes friction.

Stack Design
The event was intentionally structured so each participant played a distinct role.

- **Anchor partners** provided purpose and legitimacy:

Toy-for-Tots, the Boys & Girls Club, and a local church served as the beneficiaries and coordinated toy collection and distribution.

- **Activation partners** made the event operational:

The two teams supplied players and coaches, ran game operations, and handled concessions. A small group of sponsors covered the stadium rental, allowing the event to operate without charging admission.

- **Amplification partners** extended awareness:

All participating organizations promoted the event through their own channels using shared materials. No one carried the messaging alone.

Each group contributed what it already controlled. No role overlapped another.

With the stadium secured and costs covered, the event was positioned as a toy drive rather than a revenue event. Fans were invited to attend, with new, unwrapped toy donations accepted but not required for entry.

There was no paid advertising. Promotion happened through the collective reach of the participating organizations—teams, charities, sponsors, players, coaches, and staff—each sharing the same message through channels they already controlled.

At the gate, the beneficiary organizations managed collection and coordination. Inside the stadium, the teams focused on football. Concessions covered minor expenses. The structure held without requiring centralized promotion or spend.

The structure held.

The result was consistent year after year.

- Hundreds of toys were collected annually
- Multiple charities received support without competing
- Operational responsibility stayed clear
- No partner felt overextended

In the first year, the officiating crew recognized the nature of the event and chose to donate their time. They continued to do so in subsequent years. The system didn't depend on that generosity—but it had room for it.

That was the point.

When roles are clearly defined, partnerships don't compete — they accumulate.

The Partnership Stack does something most sponsorship models don't:

It reduces confusion.

Partners understand:

- Why they're involved
- Where they fit
- What success looks like

That clarity builds confidence—on both sides.

In small or rural markets:

- Resources are limited
- Relationships matter
- Over-asking burns trust quickly

The stack prevents overreach.

Instead of asking one partner for everything, you:

- Ask many partners for one thing each

That's sustainable.

From Stack to System
Once the stack is in place, something important happens:

You stop selling partnerships.
You start **designing outcomes**.

That's the shift from relationship management to system leadership.

What Comes Next
If the Partnership Stack defines the roles…

Then the next question is:

How do you design partnerships so everyone wins without negotiating endlessly?

That's where clarity turns into speed.

And that's where we go next.

8 DESIGNING WIN-WIN WITHOUT NEGOTIATION

Why Clarity Replaces Haggling

Most partnerships slow down at the same point.

Negotiation.

Not because people are difficult—but because the offer is unclear.

When value is vague, everyone tries to protect themselves.
When roles overlap, everyone negotiates boundaries.
When outcomes aren't defined, everyone asks for more.

Negotiation isn't the problem.
Ambiguity is.

Traditional sponsorship models force negotiation because:

- Everyone is offered the same thing
- Value is packaged, not designed
- Outcomes are implied, not defined

Partners are left asking:

- "Is this worth it?"
- "What am I really getting?"
- "Can you do more for the same price?"

So they negotiate.

Not to win—but to reduce uncertainty.

The Shift: From Selling to Designing

When partnerships are designed instead of sold, something changes.

Instead of asking:

"What do you want for this much money?"

The conversation becomes:

"Here's the role this partner plays in the system."

Roles replace offers.
Outcomes replace benefits.
Clarity replaces negotiation.

"Win-win" is often treated like a vibe.

In reality, it's a structure.

A partnership is win-win when:

- Each side knows exactly what they contribute
- Each side knows exactly what success looks like
- Neither side needs to renegotiate mid-execution

That doesn't happen by accident.

It happens when roles are designed **before** value is discussed.

The Three Design Rules That Eliminate Negotiation
These rules appear repeatedly throughout the model.

1. Roles Come Before Benefits
When partners understand their role:

- They stop comparing themselves to others
- They stop asking for exceptions
- They stop negotiating for more

They know where they fit.

2. Outcomes Are Named Up Front
Outcomes don't have to be guaranteed.
They just have to be **defined**.

Defined outcomes:

- Reduce anxiety
- Align expectations
- Prevent scope creep

When outcomes are clear, negotiation becomes unnecessary.

3. Value Is Delivered Through the System, Not Promised Individually
In this model, value isn't promised one partner at a time.

It's produced by the system.

That means:

- No custom deals
- No side agreements
- No one-off exceptions

Customization happens inside the structure, not around it. There are no deals that sit outside the system. Partners benefit because the system works—not because they negotiated well.

When negotiation is removed, speed increases.

- Decisions happen faster
- Partnerships form more easily
- Execution starts sooner
- Relationships feel lighter

This is especially important in small markets, where over-negotiation damages trust quickly.

Case Story: When the Answer Was Already Yes

When the team announced its move to a new town ahead of a spring season, outreach had barely begun. There was no sponsorship push, no pitch deck, and no formal partnership ask circulating yet.

Before any of that happened, the local YMCA director reached out.

Traditional Expectation
A conversation like this would normally turn into a sponsorship discussion:

- Budget questions
- Benefit lists
- Term length
- What goes where
- What costs what

That's usually where momentum slows.

That didn't happen here.

The director's proposal was straightforward.

The YMCA would provide **sponsored memberships** for players and brand itself as "the official training facility for the team."

In return, the YMCA would have a presence at home games with a table for recruiting and community engagement.

The role was clear:

- Facility access and credibility on one side
- Visibility, usage, and alignment on the other

No overlap. No ambiguity.

There was nothing to negotiate.

The value exchange made sense immediately.
The role fit cleanly into the system.
The outcome was obvious to both sides.

The answer was yes.

The partnership launched quickly and operated as expected.

Players trained at the YMCA.
The YMCA gained consistent exposure and recruiting access.
There were no revisions, add-ons, or follow-up negotiations required.

The agreement held because it was designed correctly from the start.

When roles and outcomes are clear, negotiation becomes unnecessary.

Why This Scales Without Burning Relationships
Negotiation scales poorly.

Design scales cleanly.

When partners:

- Self-select into roles
- Understand expectations
- See the system working

They don't feel sold.
They feel included.

That distinction matters.

At this point, the system is clear.

But one question remains:

How do you **replicate this across seasons, partners, and communities** without starting over every time?

That's the difference between a model and a movement.

What Comes Next
If design removes negotiation…

Then the next step is obvious:

How do you replicate this system without relying on you personally?

That's how the model scales.

And that's where we go next.

9 FROM SYSTEM TO PLAYBOOK

How This Becomes Repeatable Without You

A system isn't finished when it works once.

It's finished when it works **without explanation**.

Up to this point, everything in this book has been about design:

- Designing roles instead of selling benefits
- Designing structure instead of relying on goodwill
- Designing outcomes instead of chasing money

The next step is turning that design into something others can execute.

That's the difference between a system and a playbook.

Most models fail to replicate because they depend on:

- Personality
- Relationships
- Charisma
- Experience

They work because someone knows how to make them work.

That's fragile.

A playbook removes the need for interpretation.

A playbook is not:

- A checklist
- A script
- A manual

A playbook is a **sequence of decisions**, made in the right order, using the same logic every time.

It answers three questions:

1. What do we look for?
2. How do we design the role?
3. How do we activate without negotiation?

Everything else is secondary.

The Four Decisions That Make the System Portable
Every successful replication follows the same decision path.

1. Identify the Distribution Layer
Before asking for anything, identify where:

- Attention already gathers
- Timing already exists

Trust already lives
In my studies, this was sports.

In other environments, it might be:

- A school
- A church
- A community organization
- A recurring event

If there's no distribution layer, stop.

2. Inventory What You Already Control

This is not a brainstorming exercise.

It's an inventory:

- Channels
- Access
- Facilities
- Equipment
- Relationships
- Credibility

If you can't name it, you can't use it.

3. Design Roles, Not Requests

This is the most important step.

Instead of asking:

"Would you sponsor us?"

You design:

"Here's the role this partner plays."

A role has:

- A clear function
- A defined contribution
- A visible outcome

If the role is clear, the decision is easy.

4. Route Value Through the System

Value is not handed out individually.

It flows through the system:

- One activation serves multiple partners
- One effort produces multiple outcomes
- One role reinforces others

This is how small inputs compound.

Why This Works for New Operators

This playbook doesn't require:

- Capital
- Experience
- Status

It requires:

- Observation
- Discipline
- Restraint

Those are learnable.

That's why this model scales down as easily as it scales up.

Case Story: When Discipline, Not Design, Determines Replication

Over the years, there were multiple attempts to hand off parts of the system to others—staff, partners, or operators who wanted to replicate what was working.

The structure was explained.
The sequence was clear.
The logic made sense.

No one was asked to invent anything new.

In each case, the same thing happened early on.

The system was followed closely at first:

- Roles were defined
- Value was routed through the structure
- Money was not the starting point

Initial momentum appeared quickly.
Early results were visible.

On paper, the handoff looked successful.

As long as the structure was followed, outcomes were predictable.

- Partners responded positively
- Conversations moved faster
- Resistance was manageable

Nothing felt forced.
The system did the work.

Then pressure showed up.

It usually took one of a few forms:

- Someone questioned why things weren't being done "the usual way"
- Comparisons to other programs or trends crept in
- Progress felt slower than expected
- Resistance triggered impatience

At that point, discipline slipped.

Small deviations followed:

- A shortcut here
- A concession there
- A return to cash-first thinking "just this once"

Each change felt reasonable in isolation.

Collectively, they broke the system.

Once discipline was abandoned, results stalled.

Not because the structure stopped working—but because it was no longer being used.

The same pattern repeated:

- Momentum faded
- Confidence dropped
- Old habits returned

The system wasn't taken to the finish line.

The failure point was never understanding.
It was tolerance.

Tolerance for:

- Discomfort
- Resistance
- Not looking like everyone else
- Letting structure work before judging it

The system didn't require creativity.
It required patience.

A system doesn't fail under pressure.
It fails when discipline breaks before the system has time to work.

Fragile vs. Durable

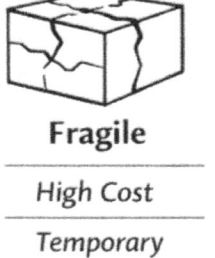 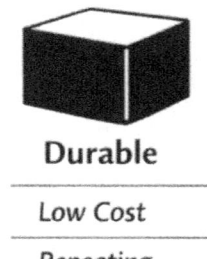

Fragile	Durable
High Cost	Low Cost
Temporary	Repeating

The Shift That Makes This Sustainable
At this stage, something changes.

You stop thinking:

"How do I make this work?"

And start thinking:

"How do I make this obvious?"

That shift is what allows
:
- Delegation
- Expansion
- Continuity

It's also what protects the system from burnout.

A playbook isn't rigid.

It's consistent.

Different environments will:

- Change the inputs
- Adjust the timing
- Alter the scale

But the sequence remains the same.

That's how you know it's a system.

From Playbook to Culture
When a playbook is used repeatedly, it becomes culture.

People stop asking:

- "Can we do this?"
- "Is this allowed?"

They start asking:

- "What role fits here?"
- "What asset are we not using yet?"

That's when the system outlives the playbook.

What Comes Next

At this point, the reader has everything they need.

What remains is not instruction, but perspective.

The final chapter isn't about what to do next.

It's about what becomes visible **once you stop leading with money**.

That's where we end.

10 SEEING OPPORTUNITY DIFFERENTLY

What Becomes Visible When You Stop Leading With Money

Once you stop leading with money, something subtle happens.

You don't feel smarter.
You don't feel bolder.
You don't feel like you've unlocked a secret.

You start noticing things you used to walk past.

The Shift Isn't Strategic — It's Perceptual
Most people believe opportunity is scarce because money is scarce.

That assumption shapes everything:

- What they pursue
- What they ignore
- What they believe is "possible"

When money becomes the first filter, most ideas die before they're examined.

When money is removed from the front of the conversation, opportunity expands.

Not because there's more of it — but because you can finally see it.

Once you understand this system, you begin to notice:

- Who already gathers people
- Who already controls timing
- Who already has trust
- Who already has unused capacity

These things were never hidden.

They were just invisible under cash-first thinking.

The Difference Between "No Budget" and "No Leverage"

"No budget" sounds like a dead end.
"No leverage" actually is one.

Most people confuse the two.

Budget is a resource.
Leverage is a position.

This book has been about building position before asking for resources.

When you hold leverage:

- Money becomes optional
- Partnerships become easier
- Resistance becomes manageable

Seeing opportunity differently often feels like hesitation.

Not because the idea is wrong — but because it doesn't look familiar.

Cash-first thinking has social proof.
Role-first thinking does not.

When you stop leading with money:

- You look slower at first
- You sound different
- You resist shortcuts others expect

That discomfort isn't confusion.
It's recalibration.

At this point in the book, the reader should recognize patterns:

- The same types of partners appear
- The same objections surface
- The same breakpoints show up
- The same discipline is tested

This isn't coincidence.

It's the system revealing itself.

Once you see the pattern, you stop chasing individual wins.
You start designing repeatable outcomes.

Before, an idea might have sounded good but felt unrealistic.

Now, the question changes.

Instead of:

"How much would that cost?"

You ask:

"Who already has what this requires?"

This question is often misunderstood as asking for favors. It isn't. Donation creates obligation; exchange creates sustainability. The goal isn't to shift cost—it's to design outcomes that make participation rational for everyone involved. This is a question of alignment: who already controls the required input, and how that control can be activated for mutual benefit.

Ideas stop feeling expensive.
They start feeling structural.

This Is Why the System Scales Down So Well
Large organizations struggle with this shift.

Smaller ones excel at it.

When you don't have money:

- You're forced to see differently
- You're forced to design smarter
- You're forced to partner earlier

That's not a disadvantage.
It's training.

Over time, opportunity stops feeling like luck.

Not because outcomes are guaranteed — but because inputs are understood.

You know:

- Where to look
- What questions to ask
- What roles make sense
- What discipline is required

That knowledge creates calm.

This book hasn't been teaching you how to get more.

It's been teaching you how to notice more.

Once that shift happens, execution becomes simpler — not easier, but clearer.

What Comes Next
Seeing opportunity differently changes how you think.

The next step is understanding why most people can't sustain that way of operating — even after they see it.

That's not a strategy problem.

It's a human one.

And that's where we go next.

11 WHY MOST PEOPLE MISS THIS

Permission, Posture, and Psychological Friction

By this point, the system should make sense.

Not intellectually — structurally.

If it didn't, the earlier chapters wouldn't have landed.

So when resistance shows up next, it's important to understand what it is — and what it isn't.

Most people don't miss this because they don't understand it.

They miss it because they don't feel permitted to operate this way.

Cash-first thinking is familiar.
Role-first thinking is not.

Familiarity feels like safety — even when it doesn't work.

The Moment Friction Appears
Resistance usually shows up right after early progress.

That's when:

- Someone asks for a price instead of a role
- A partner wants a shortcut
- Comparison to "how others do it" creeps in
- The pace feels slower than expected

This is the moment most people retreat.

Not because the system failed — but because it stopped feeling socially comfortable.

Cash-first models have social proof.

Everyone understands them.
Everyone expects them.
Everyone knows how to talk about them.

When you operate differently:

- You sound unconventional
- You can't point to standard comparisons
- You can't hide behind precedent

That creates pressure to conform.

For many people, that pressure outweighs results.

Permission Is the Hidden Constraint

Most people don't need better tools.

They need permission to:

- Ignore trends
- Stay patient under resistance
- Let structure work before judging it

Without permission, they abandon discipline at the first sign of doubt.

They don't say, "I'm reverting."
They say, "This isn't working."

Those are very different things.

When others question this approach, it can feel like they're questioning you.

They aren't.

They're reacting to:

- Unfamiliar structure
- Unclear categories
- A lack of quick labels

People push back hardest on things they can't easily place.

That doesn't make the approach wrong.
It makes it new.

The discipline required here isn't effort.
It's restraint.

Restraint from:

- Explaining too much
- Negotiating too early
- Adjusting structure prematurely
- Reverting to money for comfort

This kind of discipline feels passive — but it isn't.

It's active patience.

Why This Filters Outcomes
The system doesn't fail most people.

Most people opt out of the system.

They prefer:

- Immediate validation

- Familiar mechanics
- Visible activity

This model rewards:

- Clarity
- Consistency
- Staying inside the structure

That difference matters.

What to Do When You Feel the Pull
When resistance shows up, the question isn't:

"Should I change this?"

It's:

"Have I held discipline long enough for the system to work?"

If the structure hasn't been violated, wait.

If it has, restore it.

That's the only adjustment required.

Missing this system isn't about intelligence.

It's about tolerance.

Tolerance for:

- Standing apart
- Letting results speak later
- Trusting structure over reassurance

Once you understand that, resistance stops feeling discouraging.

It starts feeling diagnostic.

What Comes Next

If you can hold discipline through resistance, something shifts.

You stop operating as the executor of every outcome.
You start operating as the designer of conditions.

That's not a tactic change.
It's a leadership one.

And that's where we go next.

THE FORCE MULTIPLIER MODEL

12 FROM EXECUTION TO LEADERSHIP

What Changes When You Stop Doing Everything Yourself

Early on, execution feels like leadership.

You're in every conversation.
You solve every problem.
You carry momentum forward by force of effort.

That works—until it doesn't.

At some point, the system doesn't need more energy.
It needs **clearer design**.

The Trap of Being "Essential"
Many programs stall because the leader becomes indispensable.

Not because they want control—but because:

- They know how things work
- They've seen what breaks
- They're protecting the outcome

The intention is good.
The result isn't.

When everything routes through one person, scale quietly stops.

Why Leadership Feels Riskier Than Execution
Execution is familiar.
Leadership introduces distance.

When you step back:

- Others move slower
- Decisions feel less precise
- Outcomes aren't perfectly shaped

That discomfort isn't failure.

It's the system learning to stand on its own.

What Actually Changes at This Stage
Leadership doesn't mean doing less.
It means deciding **earlier**.

Instead of fixing problems, you:

- Clarify roles before confusion
- Reinforce structure before deviation
- Remove ambiguity before resistance

Your work shifts upstream.

The System Becomes the Source of Authority
When structure is clear, authority no longer comes from the person.

It comes from:

- The sequence
- The rules of engagement
- The design itself

People stop asking:

- "What should we do?"

They start asking:

- "What does the system require here?"

That's leadership.
Why Letting Go Feels Like Losing Momentum
In the short term, it often does.

When you stop pushing:

- Progress looks quieter
- Feedback loops slow down
- Activity becomes less visible

This is where many leaders step back in.

They mistake silence for failure.

What's actually happening is transition.

The Difference Between Control and Clarity
Control depends on presence.
Clarity doesn't.

A clear system:

- Holds its shape under pressure
- Guides decisions without supervision
- Corrects behavior without confrontation

Your influence increases as your visibility decreases.

What Delegation Really Requires
Delegation fails when people inherit tasks.

It works when they inherit structure.

If someone needs constant judgment calls:

- The system isn't finished

If someone can operate without interpretation:

- Leadership has done its job

This book has been about reaching that point.

Why This Stage Filters Leaders
Many people prefer being needed to being effective.

Execution provides:

- Immediate validation
- Visible contribution
- A sense of control

Leadership requires:

- Patience
- Trust in design
- Willingness to be less central

Not everyone wants that trade.

What Happens When the Shift Sticks
When leadership replaces execution:

- Decisions become more consistent
- Partners experience less friction
- Momentum becomes steadier

Most importantly, the system survives change.

That's the real test.

Leadership isn't about stepping away.

It's about building something that doesn't collapse when you do.

That's not a personality trait.
It's a design outcome.

What Comes Next
Once the system no longer depends on you, something unexpected happens.

It doesn't just function.
It compounds.

Not through effort—but through repetition.

That's where we go next.

13 WHEN THE SYSTEM BECOMES THE ADVANTAGE

Why This Compounds Over Time

Most people think advantage comes from scale.
But scale doesn't create strength — it amplifies it.

More money.
More people.
More exposure.

That kind of advantage is fragile.

What lasts is different.

Advantage Isn't Speed — It's Friction Reduction
At the beginning, everything feels hard:

- Conversations take time
- Partners hesitate
- Outcomes feel distant

Over time, something shifts.

Not because effort increases — but because **friction decreases**.

The system removes:

- Redundant explanations
- Repeated negotiations
- Constant re-justification

When friction drops, momentum becomes quieter but stronger.

Once partners understand the structure:

- They know where they fit
- They know what's expected
- They know what success looks like

Conversations shorten.
Decisions speed up.
Trust deepens.

Not because people like you more — but because the system is predictable.

Most organizations chase novelty.

New ideas.
New packages.
New tactics.

This system compounds through **repetition**.

The same roles.
The same sequence.
The same logic.

Each time it runs:

- Execution improves
- Confidence increases
- Outcomes stabilize

Innovation still happens — but inside the structure, not instead of it.

The System Starts Working Ahead of You
At this stage, things happen without prompting.

Partners:

- Suggest activations
- Refer others
- Anticipate needs

Not because they were asked — but because they understand the model.

This is where advantage becomes invisible.

Compounding rarely feels dramatic.

There are no spikes.
No big announcements.
No obvious inflection points.

Instead:

- Fewer problems arise
- Less energy is spent correcting
- More outcomes come from the same inputs

That's the signal.

How This Protects Against Disruption

Trends come and go.
Platforms change.
Budgets tighten.

A system built on:

- Roles
- Alignment
- Mutual benefit

doesn't depend on any single variable.

When conditions change, the structure adapts.
That's resilience.

The Difference Between Growth and Depth

Growth expands outward.
Depth strengthens inward.
This model prioritizes depth:

- Deeper trust
- Clearer expectations
- Stronger repeat partners

Depth creates optional growth.
Growth without depth creates collapse.

Eventually, something subtle happens.

You stop asking:
- "Can this work?"

You start asking:
- "How does this fit?"

The system becomes the lens through which decisions are made.

That's when it becomes the advantage.

You don't win by constantly upgrading tactics.

You win by building a structure that gets easier to run every time it's used.

That's what compounds — and what makes scale possible.

What Comes Next
Once you understand how this advantage builds quietly, the final test is scale in reverse.

Can this system work just as well for someone smaller, earlier, and less resourced?

That's where we go next.

14 SCALING DOWN IS THE PROOF

Why This Works Best Where Resources Are Tight

If a system only works when resources are abundant, it isn't scalable.

It's fragile.

The real test isn't whether something works when conditions are ideal. It's whether it holds up when they aren't.

That's where this model earns its credibility.

Why Most Models Fail at the Bottom
Most business models are designed for growth environments:

- Big budgets
- Dedicated staff
- Existing audiences
- Margin for error

When those things disappear, so does the model.

That's why early-stage operators struggle.
Not because they're incapable — but because the system they're trying to run **assumes advantages they don't have.**

This Model Was Built in Constraint
This system didn't emerge from abundance.

It emerged from:

- Limited budgets
- Small teams
- Inconsistent conditions
- Constant pressure to justify every decision

That matters.

A model forged under constraint doesn't break when resources tighten. It becomes clearer.

Why Smaller Environments Reveal Structure Faster
In small or early environments:

- Waste is obvious
- Friction is visible
- Misalignment shows quickly

There's nowhere to hide.

That accelerates learning.

If a role isn't clear, it fails immediately.
If an exchange isn't balanced, it collapses.
If discipline slips, momentum disappears.

That feedback loop is brutal — and useful.

What Scaling Down Actually Tests
Scaling down tests:

- Whether roles are truly defined
- Whether outcomes are real or assumed
- Whether partnerships are balanced
- Whether discipline exists without pressure

Large organizations can mask flaws for years.
Small ones can't.

That's why success here matters more.

Why This Works for Beginners and Small Operators
This system doesn't ask for:

- Capital
- Reach
- Status
- Permission

It asks for:

- Observation
- Structure
- Patience
- Discipline

Those are available at any level.

That's why youth programs, small businesses, and early-stage operators often execute this better than large institutions.

They have less to unlearn.

The Hidden Advantage of Starting Small
Starting small forces clarity.

You can't:

- Buy your way out of confusion
- Spend through resistance
- Hide behind activity

You have to design well.

That pressure doesn't weaken the system.
It sharpens it.

Why This Is the Real Signal of Scalability
If a model:

- Works with fewer people
- Works with less money
- Works with tighter margins
- Works without reputation

Then it's structurally sound.

Scale doesn't change that.
It just reveals it faster.

Scalability isn't proven by getting bigger.

It's proven by getting smaller — and still working.

If the system holds at the lowest level, it will hold anywhere.

What Comes Next
At this point, you, the reader, have seen:

- How the system works
- Why it holds under pressure
- What breaks it
- What strengthens it

What remains isn't instruction.

It's perspective.

The final chapter isn't about what to do next.
It's about what changes once you stop asking for support — and start designing outcomes.

That's where we end.

15 THE SHIFT THAT CHANGES EVERYTHING

From Asking for Support to Designing Outcomes

At some point, something changes.

Not in the environment.
Not in the resources.
In how you operate.

You stop asking for support.

And start designing outcomes.

Why Asking for Support Keeps You Small
Asking for support frames you as dependent.

Even when people say yes, the relationship is fragile.
It's built on:

- Sympathy
- Obligation
- Short-term goodwill

Support can disappear without warning.
Outcomes don't.

This book has been about replacing that dependency with structure.

Designing Outcomes Changes the Conversation

When you design outcomes:

- You don't pitch
- You don't persuade
- You don't negotiate

You present roles.

People aren't deciding whether to help you.
They're deciding whether the role fits them.

That shift changes everything.

Why This Works Across Contexts

The system doesn't depend on:

- Sports
- Size
- Budget
- Industry

It depends on:

- Attention
- Timing
- Trust
- Structure

Those exist everywhere.

Once you see that, the environment stops feeling limiting.
It starts feeling populated with options.

This Is Why Money Was Never the Point
Money solves problems quickly.
Structure solves them sustainably.

Leading with money:

- Shortens thinking
- Narrows options
- Hides leverage

Leading with structure:

- Expands possibility
- Reduces friction
- Creates alignment

Money still matters.
It just doesn't get to lead.

What Changes in You
As you operate this way, a few things happen quietly.

You become:

- Less reactive
- More selective
- Less impressed by tactics
- More confident in restraint

You don't rush decisions.
You don't chase trends.
You don't panic under resistance.

Not because you know the outcome —
but because you trust the structure.

Why This Is Transferable
Nothing in this book requires:

- Special access
- Credentials
- Capital
- Permission

It requires:

- Observation
- Discipline
- Willingness to operate differently

That's why it works at the beginning.
That's why it scales later.
That's why it lasts.

This wasn't a guide to partnerships.
Or fundraising.
Or sports.

It was an introduction to a different operating posture.

One where:

- You design before you ask
- You align before you spend
- You build leverage before you scale

Once that posture is adopted, tactics become secondary.

The Final Shift

Most people believe:

"Once I have resources, I can create outcomes."

This book has shown the opposite:

"When you design outcomes, resources follow — or become unnecessary."

That's the shift.

You don't need to start bigger.
You don't need to wait.
You don't need to convince anyone.

You need to look at what's already around you —
and design roles that make sense.

Once you do, momentum stops feeling forced.
It starts feeling earned.

The difference between asking for support and designing outcomes
is the difference between hoping something works
and knowing how it does.

Once you understand that,
you don't go back.

SEEING THE PATTERN

Once you understand how the systems work, they start to appear everywhere. Not as tactics or strategies, but as structural choices – moments where progress depended less on capital or permission and more on how value was aligned. What follows aren't case studies meant to prove a point. They're familiar examples, drawn from different eras and industries, that reveal the same underlying pattern at work.

Before Henry Ford became a household name, his early ventures struggled and reorganized. When he launched what would become the Ford Moto Company in 1903, production depended heavily on the Dodge brothers skilled machinists known for precision manufacturing. Ford lacked the capital to pay for critical components outright, so he structured an exchange – equity in return for capability.

That early partnership allowed the company to operate, produce, and grow at a moment when money couldn't lead. Scale came later. Structure came first. The Dodge brothers eventually leave to build their own successful brand, but their early contribution helped turn Ford from an idea into a functioning system.

For decades, stand-up comedy advanced through a narrow set of gatekeepers. A single television appearance – most notably *The Tonight Show* – could launch a career. With so few opportunities available, competition was intense. Comedians guarded access, protected spots, and treated success as a zero-sum game. Opportunity was scarce and tightly controlled.

As distribution expanded, the structure began to loosen. Platforms like **YouTube** allowed comedians to release material directly and audiences could form without permission. Momentum could build without a single defining break.

What changed wasn't talent – comedians still had to be good – but behavior. As opportunity widened, collaboration replaced competition. Led prominently by the generosity of figures like Joe Rogan, comedians began appearing on each other's platforms, sharing audiences instead of protecting access. Growth moved laterally instead of upward. Momentum compounded through participation.

The result was broader opportunity and more durable careers. Once the structure changed, success depended less on beating others to a gate and more on aligning with others – allowing reach, reputation, and audience to grow together.

In each case, the outcome wasn't created by money arriving first, nor by a single breakthrough moment. It emerged because the structure allowed participation before scale, alignment before leverage, and growth before permission. Once you know what to look for, the pattern isn't rare. It's just rarely named.

AFTERWORD

Once You See It

If you made it this far, you probably don't need to be told what to do next.

That's intentional.

This book wasn't written to hand you a checklist or a step-by-step plan. It was written so certain things start standing out to you on their own. And once that happens, you don't really go back.

Why Most People Won't Use This
Not because it's complicated.

Most people won't use this because it requires patience and discipline at moments when it feels easier to do something louder or faster.

It requires not reaching for money right away.
Not copying what everyone else seems to be doing.
Not abandoning a structure just because it hasn't paid off yet.

That's uncomfortable, especially in environments that reward activity more than clarity.

So most people will read this, agree with it, and then return to familiar habits.

That doesn't mean the system doesn't work.
It means it filters.

What Changes After This

If this book landed the way it was meant to, you'll notice a shift in how you look at things.

You'll stop asking:

- "Who can help me?"
- "How do I get funding?"
- "What do I need permission for?"

And start asking:

- "What's already here?"
- "Who already controls what this requires?"
- "What outcome would make this make sense for them?"

Nothing dramatic happens right away.

But internally, you're no longer waiting for alignment.
You're designing it.

This Was Never About Sports
Sports just made the mechanics easier to see.

The same principles apply to:

- Small businesses trying to grow without burning cash
- Entrepreneurs getting something off the ground
- Youth programs that are always underfunded
- Community organizations trying to do more with less

The environments change.
The principles don't.

Wherever people, attention, timing, and trust exist, this way of operating fits.

Confidence Comes First
One quiet outcome of operating this way is confidence.

Not hype. Not motivation.

The kind that comes from knowing:

- What actually matters
- What's optional
- What breaks the system
- What strengthens it

That confidence usually shows up before money does.

And when money does arrive, it's clearer where it belongs — and where it doesn't.

Where This Breaks
If this system fails, it usually doesn't fail when things are hard.

It fails when things start to work.

That's when people get impatient, distracted, or eager to expand. They add complexity or loosen the discipline that created momentum in the first place.

That pattern shows up at every level.

The difference is whether the structure stays in charge — or gets overridden.

Seeing It in the Real World
Once you understand this, you start noticing it everywhere.

Take a company like Costco.

Most people talk about Costco in terms of size or pricing. What actually makes it work is structure. They don't try to be everything to everyone. They design outcomes that make participation make sense for suppliers, employees, and customers — and then they protect that structure.

Before, you might have just seen a successful retailer.

Now, you can see the system doing the work.

This wasn't a book about partnerships.
Or fundraising.
Or growth.

It was about how to operate without relying on luck, favors, or permission.

Once you adopt that posture, tactics matter less. Money matters less at the beginning. And scale stops feeling mysterious.

One Last Thing
Most people assume success at higher levels looks completely different.

In reality, it usually looks simpler.

The same principles repeat.
The same discipline applies.
The same structures hold.

This book wasn't meant to inspire you.
It was meant to remove confusion.

Once that's gone, what you build next is up to you.

ABOUT THE AUTHOR

The author is an operator, not an academic.

For more than two decades, he has built and led community-based sports organizations, designing partnerships that allowed programs to grow without relying on large budgets, institutional funding, or traditional sponsorship models. Across multiple markets and seasons, he developed systems that aligned businesses, organizations, and communities around shared outcomes – often in environments where cash was limited, timelines were compressed, and expectations were high.

His work has involved launching teams, building partnerships with local and national brands, supporting youth programs, and operating within real constraints that don't appear in textbooks or pitch decks. The methods described in this book were not learned in classrooms or consulting frameworks – they were formed through execution, iteration, and years of real-world application.

This book reflects that perspective. It does not argue theory or prescribe tactics. It documents patterns that consistently worked when money couldn't lead, permission wasn't available, and outcomes still mattered. The systems described here are designed to be practical, repeatable, and grounded in how organizations actually function – not how they are expected function on paper.

The author continues to develop scalable, community-driven sports models built on collaborative exchange and durable partnerships.

THE FORCE MULTIPLIER MODEL

Made in the USA
Coppell, TX
27 January 2026